DECORATIVE
TASSELS & CORDS

DECORATIVE TASSELS & CORDS

EFFIE MITROFANIS

Kangaroo Press

Acknowledgments

My grateful thanks to:

My husband Memo and my daughters Helen and Maria for their encouragement and support

DMC Needlecraft Pty Ltd, 51-55 Carrington Road, Marrickville NSW 2204, for supplying threads and wooden candle cups used in this book

Lee Sincic for photography

My editor Anne Savage for her skills in bringing this book together

My friend Eileen Gale for her assistance with proofreading

Louise Savins for the ceramic pot shown on page 2

Fiona Robinson for painting the wooden moulds in the chapter on sculptured tassels

Lugarno Craft Cottage, 243 Belmore Road, Riverwood NSW 2210, and

Simply Stitches, 31 Albert Avenue, Chatswood, NSW 2067, for supplying wooden moulds

Photography - Lee Sincic
Stylist and designer - Effie Mitrofanis

Cover photograph: Tassels amongst gum leaves and rosewood platter. Basic tassels with mesh hood (page 15) are decorated with bullion knots and French knots (page 13). The holding cords are tied with six 2 m (2 yd) lengths of matching thread and tied at intervals with knots (page 10). Threads used are DMC Cébélia crochet cotton no.10, colour 619 natural, and DMC stranded cottons. The carved natural-edged Australian rosewood platter was created by Ted Wittingham of Whitts Patch via Bathurst, New South Wales.

Title page: These delightful tassels decorated with twisted cords made from stranded cotton will compliment any interior. Basic tassels (page 14) 11 cm (4¼") long are each made with half a ball of DMC crochet cotton size 20, colour 619 natural. The neck is wrapped for 1 cm (½") with 3 m (3 yds) of the same thread. A twisted holding cord (page 17) is made from seven 2 m (2 yd) lengths of DMC stranded cotton, colours 991 green and 816 red, and the knotted end finished off by method 5.2 on page 19. A decorative twisted cord made by five 2 m (2 yd) lengths of matching stranded cotton, knotted and finished off by method 5.1 on page 19, is wound around the tassel and stitched in place with matching sewing cotton. Ceramic pot by Louise Savins of Ballina, New South Wales.

Reprinted in 1996
First published in 1995 by Kangaroo Press Pty Ltd
3 Whitehall Road Kenthurst NSW 2156 Australia
P.O. Box 6125 Dural Delivery Centre NSW 2158
Printed in Hong Kong by South China Printing Co. (1988) Ltd

ISBN 0 86417 738 0

CONTENTS

INTRODUCTION

Decorative Tassels and Cords provides detailed instructions for a wide variety of simple tassels and cords. The book is aimed particularly at the novice tassel maker. It not only shows the tassels and cords in use but includes specific step-by-step instructions on how to easily vary the effects in different tassels and cords and - very importantly - how to finish off and attach them. The book also looks at the various useful applications for each design.

All the tassels and cords in this book are shown being used in specific ways, but they may be adapted for many other purposes. Think of using tassels on bags, boxes, brooches, cakes, chatelaines, clothing, curtain tie-backs, cushions, cylinders, jewel boxes, door and window curtains, earrings, fan trimmings, fresh and dried flower arrangements, gift wrappings, hats, hair ornaments, jewellery, keys, lampshades and light fittings, mobiles, pens and pencils, purses, reticules, scissors, shoes, toys, pouches, utility, tote or work bags, window blinds - what else can *you* think of?

Most people just starting out in the gentle art of tassel making are surprised at the ease with which the skills may be learned and at the very short time it takes to make these lovable little baubles.

Opposite page:
Basic tassels incorporating twisted holding cords with a hidden join in the head are made by a variation of method 5.4 (page 21). In contrasting decor colours of DMC coton perle no.5 or 8, they make delightful serviette rings on their own or attached by a lark's head knot (page 12) to metal rings

Basic tassels 4 cm (1³/₄") long made with DMC coton perle no.8, colour 991, and DMC *Fil or clair* gold, incorporate twisted holding cords with a hidden join in the head made by a variation of method 5.4 (page 21). The skirts of the tassels are not cut but pulled out to create a fan effect

METHODS AND TECHNIQUES

Materials and equipment

All you need to make tassels and cords:
- thick cardboard or matboard for card patterns
- sharp pair of scissors
- Stanley knife or craft knife for cutting cardboard
- metal rule to use with the knife
- pencil
- tape measure
- pins
- small pair of pliers for pulling needles through difficult situations
- threads and yarns
- polystyrene balls, various sizes

Needles:
- tapestry needles, assorted sizes, 16-24
- sharps needles, assorted sizes
- rug needle or knitter's needle with a large eye

Specific materials required are listed for each project.

Glossary of terms

Holding cord   A length of yarn, either plain or decorative, which ties, holds together and is used to attach the tassel.

Head   That part of the tassel above the neck.

Neck   The tied and knotted part of the tassel which holds the yarn intact and separates the head from the skirt.

Skirt   The yarn which hangs below the neck of the tassel.

Scale   Refers to the size of the tassel. This differs depending on the length of the tassel, the thickness of yarn, and the number of times the yarn is wound around a card pattern.

Card pattern   A piece of firm cardboard cut to a desired measurement around which the yarn is wound to form the head and skirt of the tassel.

Useful knots and stitches

Knots

Knots are used to tie the tassel. The following are the easiest and most useful:

Overhand (single knot)
This common, well-known knot, used as an initial 'stopper' prior to more secure fastenings, appears on the left in the photograph.

Left to right: Overhand (single) knot, double (granny) knot and overhand knot on cords

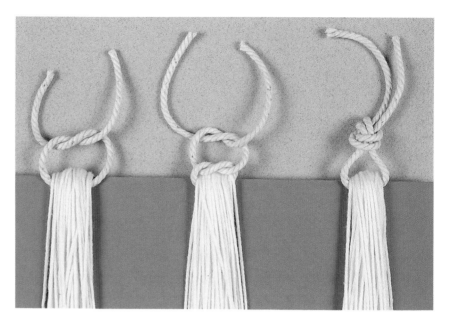

1. Place the right end of the yarn over the left end of the yarn to form a loop.
2. Pass the right hand end behind the loop, under and forward through the loop, pull firmly.

Double (Granny) knot

This commonly used knot, shown in the centre of the photo, is made when two overhand knots are tied together. The tendency for this knot to slip a little is an advantage in tassel making as it allows knots to be tightened.

Overhand knot on cords

Overhand knots (right of photograph) are often used to decorate cords or to conceal joins. They are constructed in the same way as an ordinary overhand knot, with a needle being used to hold the knot while it is being placed in position. Remove the needle and tighten the knot. Project 1 on page 25 features decorative overhand knots on the holding cords.

Double tie and wrap

This technique gives an easy way to control the ends of the yarn when wrapping short distances such as tassel necks.
1. Cut a piece of yarn approximately 46 cm (18") long and tie it around the neck of the tassel in an overhand knot. A longer yarn will be required if wrapping a width greater than 1 cm ($^3/_8$").
2. Turn the tassel over and tie a second overhand knot.
3. Hold the tassel and one of the ends of the neck wrapping yarn in your left hand (right hand for left-handers). Wrap the other tail end of the wrapping yarn very firmly in a clockwise direction for approximately 1 cm ($^3/_8$"), finishing at the head end of the neck. Take the other end and wrap it very firmly in an anti-clockwise direction on top of the first wrap, again finishing at the head end of the neck.
4. Thread the yarn ends one at a time into a tapestry needle and take the

Double tie and wrap

Steps 1 (left) and 2 (right)

Double tie and wrap

Step 3

Double tie and wrap

Step 4

needle and yarn into the tassel behind the neck and down into the skirt of the tassel. Trim the ends.

Lark's head knot

This useful knot allows tassels to be attached and easily removed from objects such as keys, scissors and knobs.

Follow the steps in the photograph showing the loop of a tassel being attached to a pair of scissors.

Lark's head knot:
Top - Take loop of holding cord around scissors handle (or curtain rod)
Middle - Insert tassel through the loop
Bottom - Tighten to form the knot

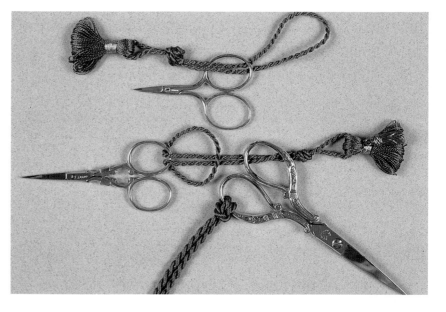

Stitches

Buttonhole stitch

A stitch created simply by taking a loop of thread behind the needle.

It is easier to add decorative stitches to tassel heads covered with a mesh hood. (Refer to Method 2 on page 15.)

Buttonhole stitch decorating the holding cord adds texture. Start by taking the needle and thread up through the skirt of the tassel, then buttonhole stitch around the holding cord. Allow the end of the thread to blend with the other threads (or core). A new thread is started by allowing its end to blend with the core; recommence buttonhole stitching through the last loop. The ends may be concealed with an overhand knot (page 10)

French knot

1. Bring a tapestry needle and thread through the skirt and out above the neck. Take a small stitch into the tassel without bringing the needle out. Make one wrap around the needle with the thread, holding it in place with the thumb.

2. Pull the needle and thread through the wrap and finish off by taking the needle back into the head close by.

French knots (left) and bullion knots (below) stitched to the head and neck of a tassel create unique and colourful accessories or displays, as shown on the cover

Bullion knot

1. Bring a tapestry needle and thread through the skirt and out above the neck. Take a stitch approximately 1 cm (³/₈") long into the tassel, pushing out as much of the needle as possible, without bringing it right through.

2. Wrap the thread six or more times around the needle, not too tight and not too loose.

3. Holding the wrapped threads down with the thumb, pull the needle and all the thread through the wraps, then lift the thumb off. Take the needle back down into the second hole made in step 1 and pull the thread through.

METHOD 1 **Basic tassel in three easy steps**

Materials
DMC Cébélia crochet cotton no.10 ecru
DMC stranded cotton 3765 blue

Following the photograph from left to right:
1. Wind crochet cotton sixty times around a card pattern 7 cm long by 5 cm wide (2³/₄" x 2"). Cut three lengths of stranded cotton 1 m (1 yd) long and thread them together through a large tapestry needle. Pass the needle and thread between the tassel and card, remove the needle and double the yarn, pulling it firmly in place at the top of the card.
2. Tie the top with a firm double knot. Remove the tassel from the card by placing the card sideways on a table and pushing the bunch of threads gradually off the card.
3. Tie the neck with a length of stranded cotton 40 cm (16") long as follows:
(*a*) Lay the tassel onto the thread and tie a single overhand knot. I find it easier to lay the thread across my knee and place the tassel in position on top of the thread.
(*b*) Flip the tassel over and tie another overhead knot on the other side and tighten. This knot is called a double tie and wrap and is shown in more detail on page 10.
(*c*) Holding the tassel and one tie in the left hand (right hand for left-handers), wrap the neck towards the skirt for about 4 mm (¹/₄"), laying the wrappings tightly side by side and then wrapping tightly again back to the top of the neck.
(*d*) Using a tapestry needle, stitch each end of the ties behind the neck to blend into the skirt of the tassel.
(*e*) Cut and trim the end of the skirt with a very sharp pair of scissors. The finished tassel is shown on the right of the photo.

METHOD 2 Basic tassel with mesh hood

This favourite tassel is created with the simple buttonhole stitch.

This favourite tassel is created with the simple buttonhole stitch and made with DMC Cébélia crochet cotton no.10, colour 619 natural, and DMC coton perle no.3, colour 597 light blue

Steps 1 to 3

1. Wind thread one hundred times around a card pattern 10 cm long by 5 cm wide (4" x 2"). Cut two lengths of yarn 1 m (1 yd) long (here I've used coton perle no.3), and thread them together through a large tapestry needle. Pass the needle and thread between the tassel and card, double the yarn and remove the needle.

2. Tie the top with a firm double knot. Remove the tassel by placing the card sideways on a table and pushing the bunch of threads gradually off the card.

3. Tie the neck with a piece of thread 30 cm (12") long, wrapping twice and tying with a double knot, then trimming the ends to the length of the tassel.

4. Begin the buttonhole stitch by taking a needle threaded with approximately 1.5 m ($1^1/_2$ yd) of yarn up through the skirt and out just above the tied neck.

5. With the head of the tassel held towards you make about ten to twelve buttonhole stitches around the neck tie, evenly spaced and approximately

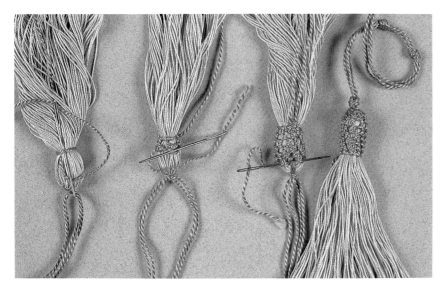

Steps 4 to 6, with finished tassel on the right

2 mm ($^1/_{10}$") apart. When you reach the first stitch, stitch into it, and keep on stitching into the previous row, spiralling up to the holding cord. As the head curves in to the top, tighten the tension on the buttonhole stitches rather than decreasing the number of stitches.

6. Finish off the remaining thread by running it around the top row like a drawstring, then pulling up the thread and taking it down into the skirt.

Creating an open mesh

Work buttonhole stitches loosely and run-stitch the last row before reaching the holding cord. This will stretch the mesh and open it up.

Running out of thread

Should your thread run out before you have finished buttonhole stitching, leave the end of the yarn unfinished while you thread a new needle and yarn up through the skirt of the tassel, bringing it out through the last worked loop. Continue buttonhole stitching with the new thread and then go back and finish off the remaining short length, taking it back down into the skirt of the tassel.

METHOD 3 Hand-made twisted cords

Length of thread required

A general rule of thumb when measuring thread to make a cord is to take a piece four times the length of the required cord. Note that thick and thin threads twist differently, so always allow a little extra length which can be trimmed later. Thick cords twist fewer times, and more quickly, than thinner cords.

After a little practice with short cords you may like to try much longer cords. If you don't haave a helper, hook the yarn around a wardrobe key or door knob and place a chair at the halfway point to stabilise the coiled yarn.

Making the cord

Double the yarn by hooking it over a door knob or door key. Twist the doubled cord between thumb and index finger until it is tightly coiled. Holding the end in one hand, double the cord and hold it taut with the other hand at the halfway point. Let it twist back on itself and tie an overhand knot at the end to prevent unravelling.

Plaited cords

Divide the threads of the holding cord into three groups and repeat the following two steps to create a simple plaited cord:
1. Take the outside right group of threads to the centre.
2. Take the outside left group of threads to the centre.

Variation

Combine three different weights of threads, cords and/or ribbons for the holding cord, divide them into three different groups, then plait them together to create an attractive textured cord. The cord can be varied in many ways, depending on the combination and scale of the threads, cords and ribbons you choose.

Hand-made plaited cords

METHOD 4 Machine-made twisted cords

Twisted cords can be made very quickly using a sewing machine. The easiest method is to utilise the bobbin winder situated on the top of some sewing machines. You also need the kind of bobbin which has holes in it.

Threads and yarns

Most threads and yarns are suitable for machine twisting. Experiment with different weights and thicknesses to achieve the result you want. Don't throw away the experiments - keep them in a bag to use for gift wrapping.

Length of thread required

A general rule of thumb when measuring thread to make a machine-twisted cord is approximately three times the required finished length of the cord. Note that thick and thin threads twist differently, so always allow a little extra length which can be trimmed later. Thick cords twist fewer times and more quickly than thinner cords.

After a little practice with short cords you may like to try much longer cords. If you don't have anyone to help you, hook the yarn around a wardrobe key or doorknob and place a chair at the halfway point to stabilise the coiled yarn.

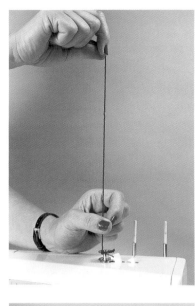

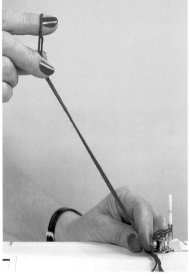

Making a plain twisted cord

Note: When twisting longer cords you may need to compensate by adding extra twists by hand on the end away from the machine, in the same direction that the cord twists, as there are more twists closer to the bobbin than a greater distance away.

Making a plain twisted cord

Before starting to twist the cord make sure that you have a pair of scissors handy near the machine.

1. Using a skein of DMC six-stranded cotton measure off three 1 m (1 yd) lengths of yarn. Place the three lengths together side by side and thread one end through a hole on the bobbin. Tie in place with an overhand knot and engage the bobbin winder.

Hold the cord vertically (at a right angle to the winder), using the other hand to create a loop with thumb and forefinger around the cord, near the bobbin, thus forming a channel to keep the thread from winding around the bobbin. Hold the thread slightly slack to allow for the twisting which will shrink the length of the cord. If you hold the cord too tightly you may pull the bobbin off the machine.

You will know the cord is twisted enough when little 'curls' appear in the thread near the bobbin.

2. Find the midway point with your other hand and fold the cord in two, keeping the cord taut to prevent uneven twisting. Hold the first 2 cm (1") of the folded end of the cord and allow this to twist. Move fingers along the cord for another few centimetres (inches) and let that portion twist. Allow the rest of the cord to twist gradually.

Cut the thread off the bobbin and tie all the ends together with an overhand knot. The cord is now ready for use.

Refer to Method 5 for ways to finish off and attach cords.

If you don't have a machine with a top-winding bobbin with holes, you can use masking tape to attach the ends of the cord to the outer part of the machine's flywheel and follow the same procedure.

Alternatively you can tie the thread to a doorknob and attach the other end to a power drill.

Variations of twisted cords

Barber's pole

This name is given to a bi-coloured twisted cord which resembles in effect the red and white striped pole which used to be seen outside men's barber shops.

To make a cord with this striped effect use the same method as for a plain twisted cord but start with a long length of yarn made by joining two equal lengths of different coloured yarn end-to-end with an overhand knot prior to twisting.

After twisting the cord, fold it in two at the joining knot then allow it to twist together as above.

Blended twisted cord

To create multicoloured cords blend different coloured threads together before twisting. Highlights can be created by blending metallic and shiny rayon threads together with coton perle, stranded cotton and crochet yarn.

All the cords shown in the photo below are made from lengths of stranded cotton.

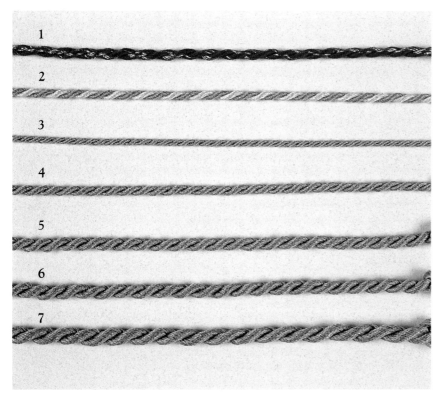

From the top:
1. 4 lengths combined with 4 lengths DMC *Fil or* gold thread by the blended method
2. 4 lengths by the barber's pole method
3. 2 lengths plain twisted cord
4. 4 lengths plain twisted cord
5. 6 lengths plain twisted cord
6. 8 lengths plain twisted cord
7. 10 lengths plain twisted cord

METHOD 5 **Finishing and attaching cords and tassels**

Quite a variety of interesting and textured hand-made holding cords may be made to finish off your tassels.

5.1 Finishing off the knotted end by stitching

Trim the knotted end by first stitching with a sharp needle and matching sewing cotton through the cord until it is secure. Wind the sewing thread around the cord four or five times, stitch through the cord again and then cut off the unwanted end, including the knot. A contrasting colour has been used here for clarity.

5.2 Finishing off the knotted end by creating a tassel

1. Make a card pattern the desired length of the tassel.
2. Thread a large tapestry needle with two or three lengths of yarn 1 m (1 yd) long.
3. Position the knot of the cord at the top of the card and wrap the new thread around the card, threading through the knot with the needle each time you wrap.
4. Remove the bundle of threads from the card and tie the neck.

Steps in making a hand-twisted holding cord

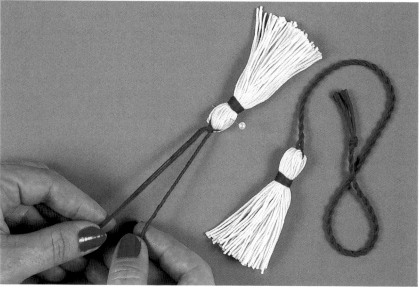

5.3 Hand-twisted holding cord

This method (shown above) makes a very tidy connection between the tassel and the holding cord as there is no stitching involved.

1. Make a tassel and tie the holding cord at the top as described in Method 1 on page 14 (which shows the holding cord as three lengths of stranded cotton 1 m (1 yd) long tied with a firm double knot). Remove tassel from the card pattern and tie the neck.

2. Secure the tassel to a flat surface with a pin - an ironing board cover is suitable. Divide the threads of the holding cord into two groups and twist each group either to the right or to the left, so long as both groups are twisted in the same direction. When both groups are well twisted, hold them taut and tie an overhand knot near the end of the threads. Unpin the tassel and allow the two groups of thread to twist together by dangling the tassel.

Tie an overhand knot just above the head of the tassel to decorate.

5.4 Twisted holding cord with a hidden join in the head

Following the steps in the photograph above:

1. Make a twisted cord by either hand or machine and thread it through the head of the tassel while it is still on the card pattern, then complete the tassel according to Method 1 or 2 (pages 14 and 15).

2. Trim the knotted end by stitching with a sharp needle and matching sewing cotton through the cord until it is secure. Wind the sewing thread around the cord four or five times, stitch through the cord again and then cut off the unwanted end, including the knot.

3. Join the two ends of the cord together to form a ring by taking the sharp needle and sewing cotton through the folded end of the cord and stitching the two together, end to end.

4. Pull the cord around so that the join is hidden in the head of the tassel.

5. Tie an overhand knot on the cord just above the head of the tassel.

Variation

Make a holding cord as described above but instead of tying the overhand knot just above the head, tie it into position approximately 3-5 cm (1"- 2") above the head.

METHOD 6 Looped fringe, rosettes, rosette tassels and ruffs

It's easy to make looped fringes to create exciting and different tassels, rosettes and fringes to decorate and trim sculptured tassels used on clothing, household items and other projects. The use of these techniques is further demonstrated in the section Finale: Sculptured tassels, on page 63.

Looped fringe

Materials
metal coathanger or narrow hairpin crochet hook
4 x 2 m (2 yd) lengths of stranded cotton, coton perle or braid to match tassel
half a cork or a flat rubber eraser
masking tape

1. Cut off one half of the coathanger with pliers to make a long U shape. Manipulate the wire so that the U is approximately 2 cm ($^3/_4$") wide. Push the two cut ends into half a cork or a rubber eraser to keep the width even and prevent the thread slipping off the hook.
2. Stick one end of thread onto the cork with a small piece of masking tape and wrap the thread evenly around the hook, starting the wrap 2 cm ($^3/_4$") away from the cork. Using the zipper foot on your sewing machine stitch along one edge of the wrapping as close to the metal as possible. Turn the hook around, adjust the zipper foot, and stitch back on top of the previous row, shown at A in the photo.
3. Remove the cork and push the fringe off the hook. The result is a looped fringe approximately 14 cm ($5^1/_2$") long, shown at B in the photo. This looped fringe may now be made into a continuous looped fringe, looped rosette tassels or rosettes.

Continuous looped fringe ruff for sculptured tassels

Make steps 1 and 2 of a looped fringe, remove the cork and push all but 2 cm ($^3/_4$") of the fringe off the hook. Replace the cork.

Wrap another lot of four 2 m (2 yd) lengths of thread around the hook and stitch it on the machine as in step 2 of the looped fringe.

Repeat until you have the required length of fringe, shown at C in the photo.

Looped rosette tassels

Make a looped fringe and cut it in half to make two tassels around twisted cords, shown at D and E in the photo.

Roll one half of the fringe firmly around the knotted, trimmed end of a twisted cord and stitch it in place, trimming loose ends, as shown at D in the photo. These tassels may be used singly or made up into bunches.

A different looped rosette tassel is made when a cord is doubled and the looped end stitched to the 'neck' of a rosette, shown as E in the photo.

Rosettes

Make a looped fringe and cut it in half to make two rosettes, shown as F in the photo. Roll one half of the fringe tightly around itself and stitch it in place with matching thread, trimming loose ends.

Push the loops flat onto the palm of the hand to spread and ruffle them. These rosettes may be used as decorative trims on sculptured tassels, clothing or other projects.

From left to right: A - looped fringe prepared on a wire hook; B - looped fringe; C - continuous looped fringe; D - rosette tassels with cord attached around the top of the rosette; E - rosette tassels with cord attached through the middle of the rosette; F - rosettes; G - a bunch of rosette tassels form the skirt of a tassel with a wooden mould covered with ready made braid

METHOD 7 **Nifty hints**

There are always nifty hints with every craft and this is also true with tassel making.

♦ Comb the tassel skirt with a tapestry needle or satay stick (skewer) after it is made to organise the threads into place.

♦ Take out kinks in the thread of the skirt by steaming it above boiling water, holding the tassel with long handled tongs to avoid burns. Comb with a tapestry needle.

♦ Divisible metallic thread is designed to be divided into individual strands, if necessary, for fine stitching. The ends of the undivided thread tend to fray, however. Fraying can be effectively prevented by applying a small amount of craft glue to approximately 1 cm (³/₈") of the end to be threaded through the needle, then pinching it to form a point.

♦ Small pliers are an effective tool for pulling needles through difficult places.

♦ Twisted cord experiments are very useful for gift wrapping. Keep them handy in a bag ready for use.

♦ Minimise tangling of thread when winding off skeins of yarn by carefully opening out the skein into a circle and placing it over your forearm while you unwind.

A sling is a great help for pulling a cord through a narrow hole. The sling can be a piece of folded wire threaded through the end of the cord. It can also be a length of yarn threaded through a tapestry needle which is taken through the end of the cord and then knotted. After the cord has been threaded into position the thread is cut and the needle and thread removed.

Nifty instant skein tassels
Make instant tassels from skeins of stranded cotton or rayon thread:
1. Fold skein in half, placing the hanging cord under the centre fold and tying with a knot to hold it in place.
2. Tie the neck, remove the bands from the skein, trim the skirt and the tassel is ready to go!

PROJECT 1
Decorative tassels with knotted cords

Two different colours forming a distinctive knot on the holding cords make this very easy tassel an eyecatching ornament for any occasion.

Materials
Colourway 1
2 balls (or 3 skeins) DMC coton perle no.5, colour 347 red
1 ball or skein DMC coton perle no.5, colour 725 yellow
card pattern 11 cm (41/2") long

Colourway 2
2 balls (or 3 skeins) DMC coton perle no.5, colour 991 green
1 ball (or skein) DMC coton perle no.5, colour 347 red

Colourway 3
2 balls (or 3 skeins) DMC coton perle no.5, colour ecru
1 ball (or skein) DMC coton perle no.5, colour 930 blue

Twisted cords

Make two twisted cords from colour 725 yellow and one twisted cord from colour 347 red. Each cord requires six lengths of yarn 2 m (2 yds) long to result in a twisted cord approximately 80 cm (32") long. These three cords together form the holding cord.

Tassel

1. Make a tassel 11 cm (4¼") long, wrapping colour 347 red around the card template 250 times.
2. Push the three twisted cords between the body of the tassel and the card as holding cords.
3. Remove the body of the tassel from the card and wrap the neck with 1 m (1 yd) of matching yarn following Method 1 on page 14.

Tassel, step 4

Tassel, step 5

Finished cords

4. Holding the tassel in the palm of your hand arrange the coloured cords to lie flat and side by side on your fingers with the red on the outside and the yellow in the middle.

5. Place your thumb over the cords to keep them in place and tie an over-hand knot with the six twisted cords. The knot should rest approximately 5 cm (2") above the head of the tassel. The red cords should remain on the outside of the knot for this distinctive effect.

Stitch or trim the ends of the cords and attach the tassel to your project or hang it on its own. Refer to Method 5 on page 19 for ways to finish off cords.

PROJECT 2
Curtain Tie-back Cluster

Materials
1 ball DMC Cébélia crochet cotton size 10, colour 619 dark ecru
1 ball DMC Cébélia crochet cotton size 10, colour 841 coffee
2 skeins DMC stranded cotton colour 918 terracotta

Other colourway suggestions
2 skeins DMC stranded cotton, colour 918 terracotta *or* 315 antique rose *or*
    924 green for neck and holding cord, *combined with* 1 ball DMC Cébélia
    crochet cotton size 10, colour 619 dark ecru *or* colour 841 coffee

1 large wooden curtain ring 7 cm (2³/₄") diameter
tapestry needle, size 18 to 22
sharps sewing needle, no.10
card pattern 5 cm (2") deep

Three bunches of tassels, step 1
(see next page)

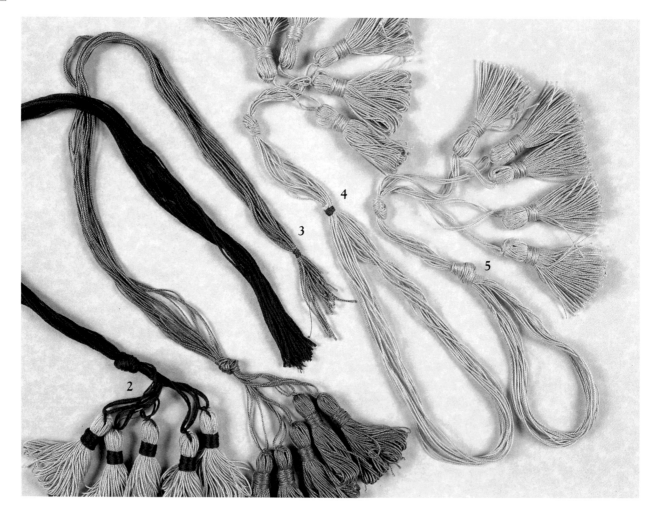

Three bunches of tassels, steps 2 to 5

Three bunches of tassels

1. Make 15 tassels following Method 1 on page 14, taking 70 wraps around the card pattern for each tassel. The holding cord is two 1 m (1 yd) lengths of thread and the neck is wrapped with a 60 cm (24") thread. Make five tassels in 841 coffee, five tassels in 619 dark ecru and five tassels in 619 dark ecru with the neck and holding cord in colour 918 terracotta.

2. Group the tassels into three separate colour bunches. On each bunch tie the holding cords together in an overhand knot approximately 5 cm (2") above the tops of the tassels.

3. Finish off the ends by stitching them together with matching sewing cotton and a sharp needle until secure. Then wind the sewing thread around the bunch of ends four or five times. Stitch through the cord again and trim off excess, as described in Method 5.1 on page 19.

4. Fold the end of each holding cord over to form a loop and attach it to the holding cord by stitching and wrapping it approximately 5 cm (2") above the single knot made in step 2.

5. Tie an overhand knot over the join made in step 4.

6. Attach each bunch of tassels to the wooden ring using the lark's head knot shown on page 12.

Tie-back cords

Make two twisted cords, one in colour 619 dark ecru and one in colour 814 coffee.

You will need 10 lengths of thread 2 m (2 yds) long for each cord. These measurements will result in a cord approximately 71 cm (28") long.

Fold each twisted cord in half to double it and attach each one to the wooden curtain ring with a lark's head knot and then tie it around the curtain to hold it in place.

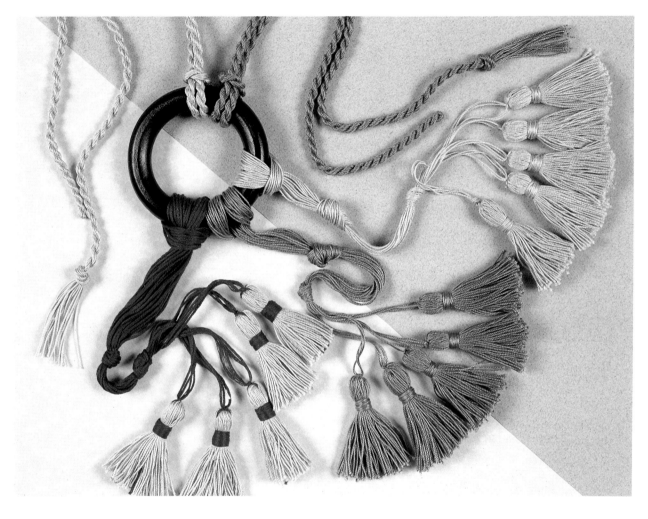

PROJECT 3
Home decor tassel in counterchange

Light and dark colours which change roles are the feature of this large tassel which may be hung anywhere in the home, for example, on a bed post, your dressing-table mirror, a curtain rod, dresser door or drawer, a door knob.

Follow the four-step sequence set out in the instructions, making the body of the tassel first in colour 1 with twisted holding cords and a wrapped neck, then making the eight hanging tassels from colour 2. The next step is to stitch a decorative mesh in colour 2 over the wrapped neck. Lastly attach the eight hanging tassels.

Materials
1 size 18 tapestry needle

Tassel body (colour 1)
1 x 50 g ball DMC Cébélia crochet cotton no.5, colour 712 cream (*or* 1 x
    50 g ball DMC Hermina knitting and crochet cotton, colour black)
card pattern 16 cm (6½") square

Eight hanging tassels (colour 2)
1 x 50 g ball DMC Hermina knitting and crochet cotton, colour black (*or*
    1 x 50 g ball DMC Cébélia crochet cotton, no.5 colour 712 cream *or*
    10 skeins DMC coton perle no.3, colour 498 red)
1 card pattern 10 cm x 25 cm (4" x 10")

Tassel body

1. After reserving 5 m (5 yds) of colour 1 for the neck, wrap the rest of the ball of yarn around the 16 cm (6½") square card pattern.
2. Make two cords from colour 2 by twisting two bundles of six 2 m (2 yd) lengths to yield twisted cords approximately 68 cm (27") long. Follow Method 3 or 4 on page 16 or 17.
3. Pass the two twisted cords between the tassel and the card pattern and double them, then tie a firm double knot at the top of the tassel.
4. Push the tassel off the card and wrap the neck for a width of 2.5 cm (1"), burying the ends with the tapestry needle behind the neck and into the skirt. Refer to Method 1 on page 14. Because the tassel is so fat you may have to pull the needle through with pliers.

Eight hanging tassels

Make eight basic tassels with wrapped necks using the 10 cm (4") card pattern, following Method 1 on page 14. Use two 60 cm (24") lengths of the same yarn to tie the tops of the tassels and 1 m (1 yd) lengths to tie the necks.

Decorative buttonhole-stitched mesh neck

1. Cut a 5 m (5 yd) length of colour 2 and tie it twice around the bottom of the neck with a double knot at its halfway point so that the two ends are the same length. Thread the two ends into a size 18 tapestry needle.

2. Holding the tassel with the top towards you stitch 12 to 16 evenly spaced buttonhole stitches approximately 4 mm ($^1/_4$") apart onto the top of the wrap created in step 1. Keep the stitches fairly loose so that the mesh will open up to show the contrasting colour underneath. When it is worked with a medium to loose tension the buttonhole-stitched mesh has a certain amount of elasticity.

After stitching the first round of buttonhole stitches take the next buttonhole stitch into the first stitch and continue stitching into the previous row, spiralling up towards the top of the neck, approximately 5 to 6 rows. Don't pick up any neck wraps except in the first and last rows of the mesh, otherwise the mesh will not stretch and open out when you finish the last row of stitches. Look at the top edge of the neck wrapping in the main photo.

1   2   3

3. Take the last row of buttonhole stitches into the top edge of the neck wrapping, as well as the previous row of buttonhole stitches, to finish off. Stitch the ends off down behind the neck and into the skirt. A pair of pliers is often handy to pull the needle through.

Attaching the eight hanging tassels

1. Thread the two ends of the holding cord of the first small tassel into the tapestry needle and stitch onto the bottom of the mesh. Make a buttonhole stitch onto the loop attaching the tassel to the holding cord near the knot at the top of the small tassel, pulling the thread until the tassel is in the correct position. Make another buttonhole stitch into the top of the loop of the holding cord near the knot at the top of the small tassel, and then finish off the threads by taking them down into the body of the tassel, passing behind the neck.

2. Attach the second tassel on the opposite side of the neck.

3. Attach the next two tassels halfway between the first two so that the spaces between the four tassels are even.

4. Attach the last four tassels in the spaces between the first four tassels.

5. Cut and trim the bottom of the tassel as required.

PROJECT 4
Wool tassel

There's nothing to compare with the generous appearance and feel of this fat wool tassel sitting firmly at the corner of the cushion. First the head is prepared, wrapped and decorated. Then the body and overskirt of the tassel are made and combined. Following this the holding cord joins the head and body together while little tassels may be added around the neck for contrast.

Materials
1 polystyrene ball 5 cm (2") diameter
1 skein DMC stranded cotton, colour 437 light tan, for decorative stitching
1 skein DMC coton perle no.5, colour 437 light tan, for little tassels
10 skeins tapestry wool, colour 7327 (*or* 1 or 2 balls 8-ply knitting wool in similar shade)
12 cm (4³/₄") square card pattern for body of tassel
3 cm (1¹/₄") deep card pattern for little tassels
10 cm (4") square card pattern for overskirt
large rug needle
tapestry needle size 18
sharps needle, size 7 or 8
sewing cotton to match wool

Tassel head

1. With a pair of sharp-pointed scissors drill a hole approximately 12 mm (¹/₂") wide down the centre of the polystyrene ball.

Making the head and body of the tassel

2. Using two lengths of wool threaded through the rug needle wrap the wool through the centre hole and around the ball until covered. This takes approximately two skeins or 16 m (15 yds) of wool.

3. If desired you may run-stitch four large decorative zigzag stitches around the ball using two 1 m (1 yd) lengths of 6-stranded cotton in colour 437 together in a tapestry needle, concealing the start and finish at the base of the ball close to the hole.

Body of tassel

1. Make a tassel following Method 1 on page 14, but wrapping the neck only twice. Use the 12 cm (4³/₄") square card pattern and two skeins of tapestry wool or 60 wraps around the card.

2. Attach a holding cord made from five lengths of wool 80 cm (32") long. Tie the neck with matching wool.

Little tassels

Using Method 1 again, make and attach five tassels which have been wrapped 50 times around the 3 cm (1¹/₄") deep card pattern from one skein coton perle no.5, colour 437. Stitch the five tassels to the head of the main tassel, evenly spaced, just above the neck.

Overskirt

1. Using the 10 cm (4") square card template wrap evenly along the card for 8 cm (3¹/₄") either using four skeins of tapestry wool or making 130 wraps.

2. Thread a length of matching wool into a tapestry needle and tie it around a few wraps of wool at one end of the wraps at the top of the card, leaving a tail of thread approximately 15 cm (6") long.

Making the overskirt and joining the tassel

Take a stitch forward approximately 4 mm ($^1/_4$") and buttonhole-stitch this group together twice. Repeat this until the wraps have all been stitched across the top, finishing at the opposite end and leaving another tail the same length. Make sure you pick up all the wool when making each stitch. I have used a contrasting wool in the photograph to better demonstrate the method.

Joining the tassel

1. Remove the overskirt from the card template and tie it around the neck of the tassel with the two tail ends.
With the two tail ends stitch the overskirt to the body of the tassel at the neck, taking the needle and thread through the tassel from one side to another several times until the skirt is securely attached.
2. Take the holding cord up through the centre of the wrapped polystyrene ball, pulling the head of the tassel only part-way into the hole, where it should sit firmly. This leaves 12 mm ($^1/_2$") of the tassel head showing between the wrapped ball and the skirt for decorative purposes.
3. Separate the ten strands of the holding cord into two groups. Twist each group separately, tie a knot in the end and let the two groups twist together as shown in Method 5.3 on page 20.
Finish off the knotted end by stitching the cord with matching sewing cotton and a sharp needle, then snip off the wool knot. Take the end back to the cord near the top of the head to form a loop and stitch it to the cord. Tie an overhand knot over the join in the holding cord.
4. Attach the looped end of the holding cord to the cushion with matching sewing cotton or insert it into the corner of the cushion during the making-up process.

PROJECT 5
Rainbow carousel

A pretty rainbow carousel mobile will add character to a child's room and delight children and adults alike.

There are three easy steps to making this decorative carousel - cover the hoop with binding tape, make the cords and tassels and then combine to hang from a plastic ring.

Materials
1 wooden or plastic embroidery hoop 20 cm (8") diameter
1 packet turquoise-green bias binding
1 split-ring plastic curtain ring 28 mm (1") diameter
1 ball each DMC coton perle no.8 in colours 666 red, 742 yellow, 741 orange,
    550 mauve, 991 green, 995 blue
card pattern 3.5 cm x 12 cm (1$^1/_2$" x 5")

Hoop

Wrap the bias binding around the hoop until the wood or plastic is covered. Stitch the end with small stitches in a matching coloured sewing cotton.

Tassels

1. Prepare all twenty-five holding cords for the tassels first, referring to Method 3 or 4 on page 16 or 17. Make five twisted cords from each colour using six lengths of thread 1 m (1 yd) long.

2. Make five basic tassels from each colour following Method 1 on page 14, wrapping each tassel 70 times around the card pattern. This makes a total of twenty-five tassels. Use the prepared twisted holding cords to tie the tops of the tassels and a length of yarn approximately 50 cm (18") long to tie the neck of each tassel.

3. Finish off the holding cords with a hidden join in the head as in Method 5.4 on page 21, and graduating the lengths of the holding cords. Each colour needs five holding cords measuring finished lengths (before the knot is tied above the head) of approximately 18 cm (7"), 16 cm (6$^1/_4$"), 14 cm (5$^1/_2$"), 12 cm (4$^3/_4$") and 10 cm (4").

4. Attach each tassel to the wrapped hoop with a lark's head knot (page 12), keeping each colour together as in the photograph.

Hanging cords and plastic ring

1. Make a twisted cord from each colour using six lengths 2 m (2 yds) long.

2. Finish off the end of each cord as in Method 5.1 on page 19, ensuring that all the cords are the same length.

3. Stitch the two ends of each cord together to form a circle.

4. Position the join in the cord approximately 5 cm (2") from a folded point in the circle and tie a knot over the join.

5. Using a lark's head knot, attach the other end of each cord to the covered hoop. Place each cord close to its matching colour.

6. Unclip the plastic split-ring, slip the looped ends of all the cords onto the ring and close it.

7. Hang the mobile in position by the plastic ring or attach a twisted cord for added length.

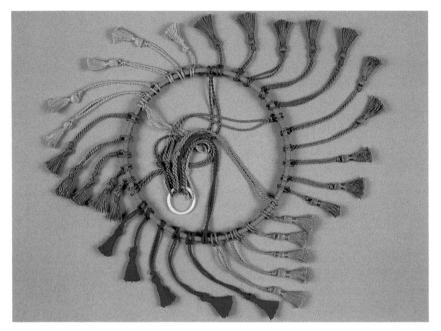

PROJECT 6
Bows and fringed tassels

Delightful bows and fringed tassels can add vitality and interest to many cushions.

Materials
1 ball DMC coton perle no.8, colour ecru
1 ball DMC coton perle no.8, colour 841 coffee
1 ball DMC coton perle no.8, colour black
1 hairpin crochet hook approximately 4 cm (1¹/₂") wide at the closed end
     (or make your own from heavy-gauge wire or a wire coathanger)
1 cushion

Bows

1. Wrap ecru and coffee coton perle 30 times each around the hairpin crochet hook, side by side to form a bunch of thread.
2. Using approximately 50 cm (¹/₂ yd) black coton perle, tie the centre of the bunch in a double tie and wrap, wrapping five or six times and tying off

Making the bows

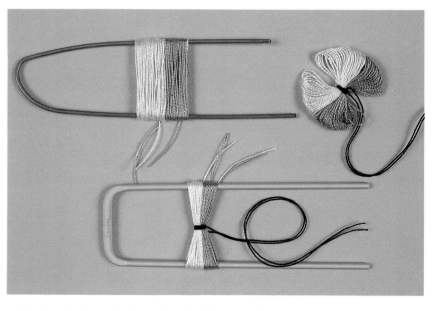

with a double knot. Refer to the double tie and wrap instructions on page 11. Trim the ends of the ecru and coffee threads.
3. Slip the bow off the hook and stitch it in place on the cushion with the black ties.

Fringed tassels

Each fringed tassel bunch is made up of three fringed tassels tied together. Make each tassel this way:
1. Make 2 bows on the hairpin crochet hook as in step 1 for Bows.
2. Cut four 1 m (1 yd) lengths of coton perle no.8 in black, ecru or coffee - this is the tying cord. Thread the tying cord around one of the tassels at the halfway point of the tying cord and tie the tassel together, wrapping and

Making fringed tassels

tying several times and finishing off with a double knot. The first tassel is now complete.

3. Take the tying cord up to the second tassel, cross the ends over, and repeat the wrapping and tying, leaving approximately 2.5 cm (1") between the two tassels.

4. Cut the two tassels off the hairpin crochet hook, pin the second tassel to a surface such as an ironing board and separate the eight strands of the holding cord into two groups of four. Twist the groups one at a time in the same direction, either to the right or to the left, until tightly twisted. Holding the twisted cords straight to prevent premature twisting, tie the ends together with an overhand knot. Allow the two groups to twist together. Tie a knot on the cord approximately 1 cm ($^1/_2$") above the head of the tassel. The first fringed tassel is now complete.

5. Make another two fringed tassels in the same way.

6. Place the three fringed tassels together and tie all the cords together in an overhand knot about 5 cm (2") above the knots on the cords.

3. Trim the ends of the cords as described in Method 5.1 on page 19 and stitch the bunch of tassels to the cushion, or insert the cords into a hole in the corner of the cushion and stitch the hole closed.

PROJECT 7
Linen tassels with pouch

Materials
30 cm Belfast linen, colour oatmeal
1 tapestry needle, size 24
DMC stranded cotton in the following colours:

Colourway 1
4 skeins colour 3803 red grape (main colour)
2 skeins colour 3807 jacaranda blue

Colourway 2
4 skeins colour 841 coffee
2 skeins colour 372 light olive

Colourway 3
4 skeins colour 3807 jacaranda blue
2 skeins colour 3812 emerald green

Bag

Finished size 24 cm x 12 cm (9$\frac{1}{2}$" x 4$\frac{3}{4}$")
1. Stitch a line of tacking thread on the fabric to mark the size of the pouch, leaving 6 cm (2$\frac{1}{4}$") of fabric all around the shape for seam allowances and ease of working. Draw pencil lines between the arrows on the graph to mark

Making the linen pouch, steps 1-4

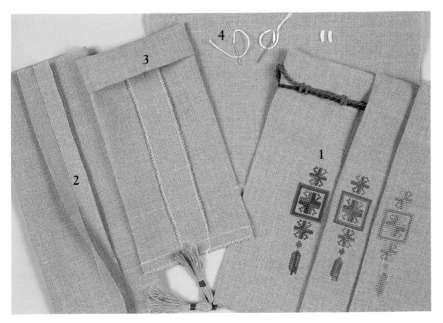

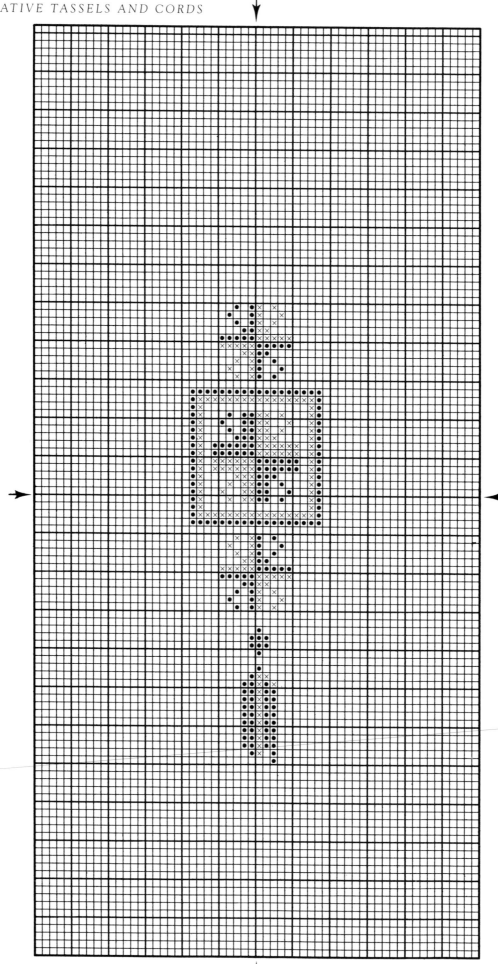

the centre. Stitch tacking lines on the fabric to mark the centre of the pouch and work the design following the graph.

Use two strands of stranded cotton in a size 24 tapestry needle and work each cross-stitch over two threads of fabric.

2. Stitch the pouch together by first folding the fabric in half lengthwise, right sides together, and pinning the seam to form the centre back join. Trim the seams to 12 mm ($^1/_2$") and overlock or zigzag stitch the raw edges. Flatten the fabric so that the seamline is at the centre back. Stitch a seam across the base of the bag, trim to 12 mm ($^1/_2$") and overlock or zigzag stitch the raw edges.

3. Turn a hem at the top of the bag by folding in 3.5 cm (1$^3/_8$"), overlock or zigzag stitch the raw edge and stitch the hem with matching sewing cotton.

4. Using six strands of stranded cotton in the main colour, make six pairs of buttonholed bars evenly spaced around the top of the pouch, starting 2.5 cm (1") down from the top. Begin each bar by making two back-stitches approximately 12 mm ($^1/_2$") long in the same two holes. Bring the needle out 3 mm ($^1/_{10}$") to the left of the first hole and stitch approximately seven or eight buttonhole stitches along the double bars of the back-stitches, but not through the fabric. Take the needle through to the back of the fabric 3 mm ($^1/_{10}$") to the left of the second hole and finish off.

The bag is now ready to be trimmed.

Twisted cord

1. Make a twisted cord from four 2 m (2 yd) lengths of colour 1, and another twisted cord the same length from colour 2.

2. Stitch the two unknotted ends together.

3. Trim the knotted ends to create a small tassel (refer to Method 5.1 on page 19).

3. Create a sling with a tapestry needle (refer to page 24) and thread the cord twice around the bag under the buttonholed bars.

4. Tie the knotted ends together and create a small tassel using Method 1 on page 14.

Tassels

Make four tassels from unravelled threads of the remaining fabric. For each tassel use 40 strands of thread approximately 14 cm (5$^1/_2$") long. Fold each group of threads in half, tie on a holding cord and make a neck using some stranded cotton in one of the colours of the cross-stitch. Attach to the corners of the bag, securing and finishing off the thread on the seam inside the bag. Trim the skirts of the tassels.

PROJECT 8
Rose bouquet tassel

The rose bouquet tassel is a delightful decorative element for weddings, confirmations or other special occasions. It is made up of three parts - foundation tassel, overskirt and roses.

Materials
DMC Cébélia crochet cotton no.10 in the following colours:

Colourway 1
1 ball white
1 ball ecru

Colourway 2
1 ball colour 223, ...
1 ball colour 224, antique pink

6 or 12 silk roses in two colours to match the chosen colourway
card pattern for tassel 14 cm (5^1/$_2$") long
card pattern for overskirt 20 cm x 16 cm (8" x 6^1/$_4$") with a window 12 cm
    x 5 cm (5" x 2") cut 3 cm (1^1/$_4$") down from the top
medium weight card pattern for overskirt 20 cm x 16 cm (8" x 6^1/$_4$") with no
    window, to be used together with the window card pattern
matching sewing cotton
sharps needle

Foundation tassel

1. Choosing one of the colourways, make a twisted cord from each colour from six 2 m (2 yd) lengths of thread. This will make a cord approximately 73 cm (29") long.
2. Using the 14 cm (5^1/$_2$") card pattern, wrap one of the colours around it 400 times.
3. Push the two holding cords between the tassel and the card pattern. Stitch the knotted ends as shown in Method 5.1 on page 19, making sure that both cords are the same length, then snip off the knot.
4. Loop one cord to make a circle and join the two ends together. Repeat with the second cord. Place the joins in the head of the tassel.
5. Remove the tassel from the card and wrap the neck firmly for 12 mm (^{1}/$_2$") with a length of thread 3 m (3 yds) long. Refer to Method 1 of Techniques on page 14.

6. Trim the skirt and comb it with a tapestry needle. Tie a knot in the cords above the head.

Overskirt

1. Place the two card patterns for the overskirt together, keeping the cards flat during wrapping and not allowing them to bow. Working with two balls of thread simultaneously, wrap approximately half a ball of each colour around the two card patterns, working backwards and forwards over a width of 12 cm (5"). Cut the balls loose from the card pattern. Remove the medium weight card pattern, leaving the thread on the window card in readiness for the next step.

2. Using the longest length of straight stitch on your sewing machine, stitch forwards and backwards five or six times onto the thread approximately 4 cm (1$^1/_2$") from the top of the card.

3. With sharp scissors cut the bottom of the skirt. Cut the card pattern away from the tassel, leaving the top to form loops. This forms a fringed skirt which is now ready to be stitched around and onto the foundation tassel.

Assembling tassel, overskirt and roses

1. Cut a 2 m (2 yd) length of yarn and wrap it around the neck. Attach six roses one at a time around the neck, trimming the wire stems with pliers.

2. Take the fringed skirt with looped end near the head and wrap it firmly in place around the neck, pinning it in place. Wrap over the fringe at the neck with 4 m (4 yds) crochet cotton for approximately 5 mm ($^1/_4$").

The tassel is now complete, with six roses. If you wish to make it look even more luxurious, attach a second row of six roses to the neck, repeating the wrapping and trimming the wire stems of the roses with pliers.

From left to right:
starting the foundation tassel;
making the overskirt; and
assembled rose bouquet tassels

PROJECT 9
Beaded pendant tassel

Materials
silk fabric 6 cm x 4 cm (2½" x 1½")in the colour of your choice
1 skein DMC stranded cotton in a colour to match silk and beads
small seed beads in a colour to tone with silk
small gold seed beads
bugle beads to tone with silk
beading needle or no.10 sharps needle
beeswax
sewing cotton to match beads

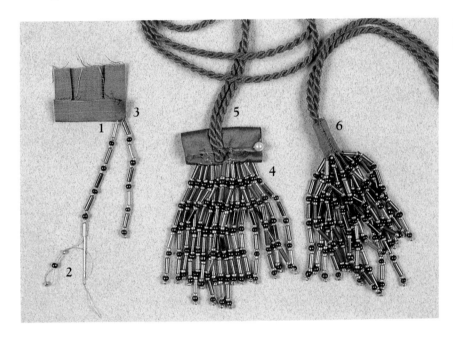

Steps 1 to 6 in making the beaded pendant

Twisted holding cord

Make a twisted cord from four 2 m (2 yd) lengths of stranded cotton. Stitch the knotted end with matching sewing cotton and snip off the knot, following Method 5.1 on page 19.

Pendant

1. Fold and press 1 cm (⅜") turnings on one long edge and both short edges of the silk fabric.

Thread beading needle with matching sewing cotton and pull the thread through a piece of beeswax to strengthen it.

Knot the end of the thread, attach it to the corner of the long folded edge

of fabric and secure with several concealed back-stitches. Make the first string of beads by threading a pleasing arrangement of bugle beads and seed beads onto the needle and thread. I used five bugle beads with one coloured bead between two gold seed beads separating each one.

2. Take the needle back up through the beads, missing the bottom bead on the string. Hold the thread firmly to avoid splitting the downward thread with the return. Missing the bottom bead on the return allows it to act as a 'stopper' which prevents the other beads falling off the thread. It is easier to pull the sewing thread by holding the 'stopper' bead while you pull.

3. Pull the sewing thread and secure it with a couple of back-stitches on the turning of the fabric. This turning will later be tucked to the inside of the pendant.

4. Attach another thirteen strings of beads along the turning of the fabric in the same manner and with the same number of beads.

Add another four strings of beads each approximately 1 cm (^{1}/$_2$") longer than the first group. There are now 18 strings of beads hanging from the silk to form a fringe.

5. Fold the silk in half and stitch the edges together with small slip-stitches. Fold the holding cord in half to form a loop and stitch the ends to the silk fabric, as shown in the photograph.

6. Roll the fabric around the cord and stitch it neatly in place.

PROJECT 10

Painted wooden mould with looped skirt tassel

White and gold threads combine with a painted wooden mould to create a stunning looped tassel.

Materials

Painted tassel head

wooden candle cups, medium and large (from craft and folk art suppliers)
gold spray paint (or folk art tube paint and brush)
PVA wood glue

Enlarge the holes in the tops of the candle cups to approximately 5 mm (¹/₄") and glue the two cups together with the smaller one on top. Spray or paint with gold.

Looped skirt

1 ball DMC Cébélia no.10 blanc
1 reel DMC rich gold metallic yarn
matching sewing cotton
sharp needle
craft or fabric glue
card pattern 4 cm (1¹/₂") deep for small tassels
2 card patterns for tassel skirt each 21 cm x 26 cm (8" x 10") with a window 19 cm x 4.5 cm (7¹/₂" x 1³/₄") cut out 6 cm (2¹/₂") from the top of one card
    (the two thicknesses of card are necessary to keep the patterns flat during
    wrapping and prevent them from bowing)
polystyrene ball 4 cm (1¹/₂") diameter

1. Make two twisted cords from eight 2 m (2 yd) lengths of Cébélia thread. They will be approximately 73 cm (29") long.
2. Make twelve small 4 cm (1¹/₂") tassels with Cébélia thread, wrapping 75 times for each tassel.
3. Tie holding cords on each tassel and tie an overhand knot approximately 10 cm (4") above the tassel. Each holding cord consists of nine 50 cm (18") lengths of thread (three of Cébélia and six of gold metallic yarn).
4. Wrap the rest of the ball of Cébélia around the two large card patterns. Make the wraps 17 cm (6¹/₂") wide over the window. Remove the plain pattern, leaving the thread on the window card in readiness for the next step.
5. Using the longest length of straight stitch on your sewing machine, make

two lines of stitching 12 mm (¹/₂") apart on the thread, working forwards and backwards five or six times as shown in the photo.

Cut the thread off the card with sharp scissors at both top and bottom of the card, and cut between the two stitched lines in the window.

6. Stitch the knotted ends of the two cords from step 1 to the larger fringe cut from the card template, and roll the fringe firmly around the cords.

Check to see if the top of the tassel will fit easily into the candle cup, allowing for the fact that more threads will be added later. If it is too tight some threads may need to be cut off.

7. Add the twelve tassels by stitching each one to the top of the fringe. When all the tassels have been stitched glue them in place and cut off excess at the top.

8. Thread the cords through the wooden head and arrange the twelve tassels evenly around the head. Bring one cord down and wind it around the head and stitch or glue the end in place just below the bottom of the wooden mould. Lift the skirt away and glue the polystyrene ball to the threads of the skirt, centrally in line with the head. (Only use glue suitable for polystyrene.)

Make a loop in the remaining cord and tie a decorative overhand knot. The tassel is now ready to be hung.

Steps 1 to 8 in the construction of a looped skirt tassel with painted wooden mould

PROJECT 11
Bunch of tassels

This bonbon is a multiple treat of two sizes of basic tassels attached to a plastic ring, combined with two wrapped polystyrene balls and finally joined with plaited cords.

Materials
2 balls each of DMC coton perle no.8, colours 311, 312, 322 blues
2 skeins DMC coton perle no.5, colour 312 blue
1 split-ring plastic curtain ring 28 mm (1") diameter
2 polystyrene balls approximately 4 cm (1½") diameter
card pattern 15 cm x 3.5 cm (6" x 1⅜")
card pattern 15 cm x 4.5 cm (6" x 1¾")
large tapestry needle
sharps needle and blue sewing cottons to match coton perle

Components of the bunch-of-tassels tassel - holding cords, the thirty basic tassels and the wrapped polystyrene balls

Holding cord

1. Make a twisted cord in each shade of the blue coton perle no.8, using nine 2 m (2 yd) lengths of thread for each. Each cord will be approximately 75 cm (30") long.
2. Place the three cords together, lining up the unknotted ends, and tying them together at the knotted ends.
3. Plait the three cords, starting at the knotted end, and stitch the ends together with matching sewing cotton.

Basic tassels

1. Make fifteen basic tassels following Method 1 on page 14, each 3.5 cm (1¾") long, taking 100 wraps for each around the card pattern. Make five tassels in each of the three colours 311, 312 and 322 for a total of fifteen. Tie

a holding cord to each tassel with a single length of matching thread approximately 50 cm (18") long.

2. Make another fifteen basic tassels Method 1, this time 4.5 cm (1¼") long with 100 wraps each around the card pattern, making five in each of the colours 311, 312 322. Tie a holding cord to each tassel with a single length of matching thread approximately 50 cm (18") long.

Wrapped polystyrene balls

1. With one end of a pair of sharp-pointed scissors drill a hole approximately 1.5 cm (½") in diameter through the centre of each polystyrene ball. Trim rough edges around the hole with sharp scissors.

2. Wrap two polystyrene balls using long double lengths of coton perle no.5, colour 322 blue, threaded together in a tapestry needle. Attach the thread by tying it through the centre hole, wrapping it through the hole and around each ball until covered. Start and finish subsequent new threads in the hole, concealed by previous wraps.

Attaching the tassels to the plastic ring, steps 1 to 4 (from left to right)

Attaching the tassels to the ring

Attach the fifteen smaller tassels to the plastic ring, alternating the three shades of blue. Following the photograph above:

1. Thread the two ends of the holding cord through a tapestry needle and take it up through the centre of the ring.

2. Make a loop, take the yarn from the top down through the ring and over the loop, forming a buttonhole stitch. Pull thread to secure tassel in place.

3. Make another buttonhole stitch on the loop attaching the tassel to the the holding cord near the knot at the top of the tassel head. Take the remaining yarn down through the tassel, trimming it to the same length as the tassel

skirt. (This technique is demonstrated using a contrasting colour.)

4. After attaching the fifteen smaller tassels tie them together as shown in the photograph to keep them temporarily out of the way for the next step.

5. Attach the fifteen larger tassels between the smaller tassels already attached to the ring. Alternate the large tassels between the small tassels, also alternating the three shades of blue. Undo the temporary tie and arrange the smaller tassels to sit in place on top of the larger tassels.

Assembling the tassel

Assembling the tassel

The components of the tassel are now ready to be joined together. First attach a sling (refer to page 24) with a large tapestry needle to the unknotted end of the plaited cord. Pull the cord through one wrapped ball, then the ring of tassels, then the second wrapped ball, and pull them firmly together. Loop the holding cord and stitch the ends with matching sewing cotton onto the cord just above the head of the upper polystyrene ball. Tie a decorative overhand knot over the join.

The tassel is now ready to be attached with a lark's head knot to a basket or knob or used decoratively in other ways.

FINALE
Sculptured decorated tassels

Dramatic sculptured tassels called *passementerie*, from the French word meaning 'trimmings', are made either with wooden moulds available in various shapes and sizes from specialty shops or with sculptured moulds made from felt, quilt wadding and pantyhose.

There are four elements to a sculptured tassel. I haven't specified threads and quantities, to encourage you to select a range of harmonious or contrasting colours to suit your own decor and style; start by making one of each element, choosing the method which appeals to you.

Sculptured tassels:
1. A sculptured mould is dressed with strips of silk fabric and then beaded. Two knots in the holding cord separate a wooden bead wrapped with DMC *Fil or* gold thread. The skirt is two looped fringes made on a card pattern (pages 51, 57, 69), with a continuous looped fringe (page 23) wrapped four times over it and underneath the head. A polystyrene ball is attached to the mould underneath the skirt to make it fatter.
2. A sculptured mould is covered with ready made cord and combined with matching holding cords and a continuous looped fringe (page 24) made with Russia braid. A fringed skirt made by the masking tape method (page 67) covers a polystyrene ball.
3. A wooden mould covered with ready made cord is topped with rosettes (page 23) and matching holding cords tied with two decorative overhand knots. The fringed skirt is made by the masking tape method (page 67) with an overskirt of rosette tassels (page 23). Rosettes are attached to the top of the skirt and the neck is wrapped with cord.
4. A wooden mould is covered with ready made cord (page 64) and a bunch of rosette tassels (page 23) is attached to the holding cord

The four elements are:

The head A moulded shape with a hole through the centre

Holding cords These hold all the elements of the tassel together and form a loop by which to hang the tassel. The trimmed ends of the holding cord are attached to the skirt and the looped ends taken up through the hole of the head with a sling (see page 22) and tied or glued into place.

Skirt Takes the form of a rolled fringe, a group of smaller tassels joined together, or both.

Meeting points and features The places where these elements meet are concealed by looped fringing, rosettes, ribbon, cords or braid.

The head

Wooden mould

Materials

- wooden tassel head
- Russia braid or thick cord to wrap around the head
  (*Note*: A small head takes about 6 m (6 yds) of braid plus an extra 2 m (2 yds) for each holding cord. A large head takes about 12 m (12 yds) of thick cord plus an extra 2m (2 yds) for each holding cord)
- 450 stainless adhesive or tacky craft glue
- wooden skewer stick

Glue the cord onto the wooden head. Start by gluing the cord onto the edge of the hole at the top, leaving a 6 cm (2¹/₂") tail of cord to tidy up gaps at the finish. Hold the cord in place with a skewer stick and allow to dry for a few minutes. Apply glue around the top of the mould for approximately 1 cm (¹/₂") and wrap the cord two or three times around the head on top of the glue, and allow it to dry. Continue applying glue and wrapping the cord around the head in sections until the head is covered, allowing time for the glue to dry between each section.

Sculptured mould

Materials

- piece of felt 12 cm x 18 cm (5" x 7")
- Aquadhere PVA glue
- 450 stainless adhesive or tacky craft glue
- 0.5 m (¹/₂ yd) quilt wadding, thin to medium thickness
- 1 pencil, knitting needle or dowel stick approximately 8 mm diameter
- 1 polystyrene ball 5 cm (2") diameter
- sewing cotton and needle
- 1 pair pantyhose (cheaper thicker quality or support hose are easier to use than sheer); cut each leg in a spiral from the top of the leg to the toe to make a single strip 4 cm (1¹/₂") wide. Wrap the strip around a cylinder to minimise rolling.

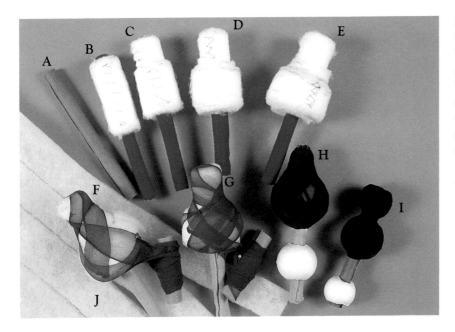

Pear shaped sculptured mould. From left to right: A - felt cylinder; B, C, D, E - the four steps in attaching wadding to the cylinder; F, G - wrapping the mould with a strip of pantyhose; H - finished mould with a polystyrene ball added at the bottom to make the skirt fuller; I - ball shaped mould (page 66); J - wadding marked for cutting into strips

Making the cylindrical tube

1. Liberally apply glue on one side of the felt.
2. Roll the felt around a pencil, knitting needle or dowel to create a cylindrical tube 18 cm (7") long, shown as A in photo. Pin ends in place. Remove the cylinder from the pencil immediately and allow it to dry for approximately twenty-four hours and become stiff. Remove the pins before the glue dries completely.

Covering the tube with wadding to create a pear shape

To create a pear shape shape with wadding, first mark the wadding with laundry marker pen and ruler, then cut into strips with sharp scissors to the following measurements:

    1 strip 9 cm x 60 cm (3" x 24")
    1 strip 6 cm x 60 cm (2³/₈" x 24")
    1 strip 5 cm x 60 cm (2" x 24")
    2 strips 4 cm x 60 cm (1¹/₂" x 24")

Results may vary depending on the thickness of the wadding and individual tension in applying it and the pantyhose to the tube. Experiment with different shapes.

1. Referring to B in the photo stitch the end of the 9 cm (3") strip of wadding to one end of the felt cylinder.

    Place the felt cylinder back on the pencil, knitting needle or dowel for easy handling and wrap the wadding very firmly around the cylinder, stretching as you wrap. Stitch the end of the wadding in place. The end where the cylinder protrudes from the wadding is the bottom of the mould.

2. Stitch the end of the 6 cm (2³/₈") wide strip of wadding to the bottom end of the previous layer, then wrap it very firmly around the previous layer and stitch the end in place, as shown at C in the photo.

4. Repeat the previous step for the 5 cm (2") wide strip of wadding, as shown at D in the photo on the previos page, and the two 4 cm (1½") wide strips of wadding, as shown at E.

Shaping the wadding with pantyhose

1. Stitch one end of the strip of pantyhose onto the wadding and start wrapping around it in a figure of eight manner (like wrapping a bandage), keeping the strip of pantyhose open and flat, wrapping firmly over and over to create the curved shape as shown at F in the photo on the previous page. It doesn't matter if the edges of the pantyhose roll slightly.
2. Keep on wrapping, across and up, diagonally, around and down, again and again, following the direction that the grain of the pantyhose takes you, smoothing over little bumps and lumps as shown at G in the photo. Stitch the end in place. It takes approximately the whole strip from one leg of pantyhose to complete the wrapping.
3. Keep the hole open at the top by stitching back the wadding and stocking. If you're not pleased with the first result unwrap it and try again. If the shape is too small or you've flattened it in places, cut more wadding into strips and apply more layers as needed to build up the volume, then re-wrap with pantyhose.

Cover the mould by stitching or gluing Russia braid or cording to it.
Note: A small head takes about 6 m (6 yds) of braid plus an extra 2 m (2 yds) for each holding cord. A large head takes about 12 m (2 yds) of thick cord plus an extra 2 m (2 yds) for each holding cord.
4. The finished mould, shown at H in the photo on the previous page, has a polystyrene ball placed over the cylinder and under the mould to make the skirt appear fuller. Drill a hole through a polystyrene ball with one end of a sharp pair of scissors and glue it to the cylinder approximately 2 cm (¾") below the mould. Only use glue suitable for polystyrene.
5. Cut off excess cylinder.

Creating a ball-shaped mould

Materials
- cylindrical felt tube 15 cm (6") long (following instructions on page 65)
- 2 polystyrene balls 4 cm (1½") diameter
- 1 polystyrene ball 5 cm (2") diameter
  pantyhose (cheaper thicker quality or support hose are easier to use than sheer); cut each leg in a spiral from the top of the leg to the toe to make a single strip 4 cm (1½") wide. Wrap the strip around a cylinder to minimise rolling.

1. Drill a hole through each polystyrene ball with a pair of sharp-pointed scissors. Attach the balls to the felt cylinder using glue suitable for polystyrene. One of the smaller balls is attached to the top of the cylinder and the larger one underneath it separated by a space of approximately 5 mm (⅜").

The other small ball is glued to the bottom of the cylinder.

2. Hold one end of a strip of pantyhose to the large polystyrene ball and start wrapping around the two top balls in a figure-of-eight manner (like wrapping a bandage), keeping the pantyhose open and flat, wrapping firmly over and over. Stitch the end in place. The finished mould is shown at I on page 65.

Holding cords

Using cords, threads and braids to match the rest of the tassel, make each holding cord from approximately 2 m (2 yds) of cording. Fold in half and stitch or wrap the ends together.

Tassels using ready made fringe as a skirt. From left to right:
1. A sculptured mould (page 64) covered with cording. A fringe of beads (page 53) over the skirt is inserted between an overhand knot in the holding cords and a simple rolled fringe skirt
2. An overhand knot is tied in the holding cords above a simple rolled fringe skirt
3. A folk art painted mould and a continuous looped fringe (page 23) are inserted between an overhand knot in the holding cords and a simple rolled fringed skirt
4. A painted wooden mould is inserted between an overhand knot in the holding cords and a simple rolled fringed skirt

Skirt

There are several ways to make a fringed skirt - using ready made fringe, making a fringe with masking tape or a card pattern. You can also make a skirt with a group of small tassels joined together, or even combine fringing and small tassels.

Ready made fringe

Approximately 50 cm (18") of ready made fringing makes up into a very quick and attractive skirt. Fringes of different lengths are sold in various looped, cut, and corded textures. The amount required will depend on the thickness of the fringe.

Wrap the fringe around the trimmed ends of the holding cord and stitch or glue in place to create the tassel's skirt.

The photo on page 68 shows four ways to use this skirt.

1. Simply tie an overhand knot in the holding cords above the fringe.
2. Take the holding cords up through a mould with a sling (shown on page 24) and tie a knot in them above the head.
3. Add a looped ruff around the top of the skirt and take the holding cords up through a mould with a sling and tie a knot in them above the head.
4. A sculptured mould covered with cording and a fringe of beads over the skirt is inserted between an overhand knot in the holding cords and a simple rolled fringe skirt.

Making a fringed skirt using masking tape

Make a fringe, finished size 20 cm (8") wide by the desired length. Wrap and secure it around the trimmed ends of the holding cord.

Materials
masking tape (low-tack stencil tape is best)
yarn/thread of your choice (use one type and colour of thread or combine
      different colours of threads, yarns and ribbon to mix and match)

To make a fringe, finished size approximately 20 cm (8") square:
1. Lay two 30 cm (12") strips of masking tape, sticky side up, on a flat surface such as a table, with a gap of 4 cm (1½") between the two strips. Tape the two ends to the table in preparation for the next step.
2. Lay threads for 20 cm (8") along the two strips of masking tape. These threads can be cut-up skeins or balls of yarn as well as any other thread you wish to include. The threads should be approximately 20 cm (8") long, measured from the centre of the gap between the two strips of tape.
3. When you've finished laying the threads, place two strips of masking tape over the threads and the masking tape laid in step 1. Remove the fringe from the flat surface.

Making a fringed skirt using masking tape: A - masking tape holds the threads together while they are machine stitched; B - fringed skirt with holding cords attached in readiness for rolling the skirt and joining it with the head; C - example of a wooden mould; D - wooden mould wrapped with cord

4. Machine stitch two or three rows of long straight stitch through all of the threads in the space between the strips of tape.
5. Cut the fringe off approximately 5 mm ($^1/_4$") above the stitching and remove the tape.
   Wrap the fringe around the ends of the holding cords and stitch or glue it in place to finish the skirt.

Fringe made on a card pattern

Make a fringe around a card pattern as shown in projects 8 and 10 (pages 51 and 57), adjusting the length of the card pattern to suit your requirements and leaving the loops intact by cutting the card away from the fringe.

Bunches of tassels

Make bunches of basic tassels or looped rosette tassels (refer to pages 14 and 23) which should be stitched or tied to the holding cord ready for assembly.

Meeting points and features

Neck ruff

To trim the neck use a looped fringe or rosettes as a ruff around the neck and the top of the head. Refer to pages 22 and 23 for instructions on how to make the looped fringe, looped tassels and rosettes.
   A looped fringe needs to be long enough to be wound around the neck three times. Stitch or glue in place and ruffle it to separate the loops.

Joining the tassel together

The head, skirt, holding cords and trimmings are now ready to be joined.

There are two ways to attach the skirt to the mould:

1. Wrap a fringed skirt around the neck of the mould and cover the join with braid, ribbon, cording or a continuous ruff, securing in place with stitching or glue.

2. Wrap a fringed skirt around the holding cords, stitching or gluing in place (stitching is preferred initially to allow for amendments or variations), pull the cords up through the hole in the mould with a sling of looped wire (see page 24) and stitch or glue into place. Decorate the join with braid, ribbon, cording or a looped fringe ruff. Tie a decorative knot or knots in the holding cords.